WHY GOD RAISED US UP

The Story of the Church of the Nazarene

RYAN GIFFIN

THE FOUNDRY
PUBLISHING®

Copyright © 2025 by Ryan Giffin

The Foundry Publishing®
PO Box 419527
Kansas City, MO 64141
thefoundrypublishing.com

ISBN 978-0-8341-4372-2

All rights reserved. No part of this publication may be reproduced, stored in a retrieval system, or transmitted in any form or by any means—for example, electronic, photocopy, recording—without the prior written permission of the publisher. The only exception is brief quotations in printed reviews.

Cover design: Caines Design
Interior design: Sharon Page

Scripture quotations marked KJV are from the King James Version.

Scripture quotations marked NIV are from the Holy Bible, New International Version® (NIV®). Copyright © 1973, 1978, 1984, 2011 by Biblica, Inc.™ Used by permission of Zondervan. All rights reserved worldwide. www.zondervan.com. The "NIV" and "New International Version" are trademarks registered in the United States Patent and Trademark Office by Biblica, Inc.™

Library of Congress Cataloging-in-Publication Data
A complete catalog record for this book is available from the Library of Congress.

The internet addresses, email addresses, and phone numbers in this book are accurate at the time of publication. They are provided as a resource. The Foundry Publishing® does not endorse them or vouch for their content or permanence.

I dedicate this book to my dear parents,
Bob and Diana Giffin.
Thanks for raising me and for raising me
in the Church of the Nazarene.

Contents

Acknowledgments	7
Introduction: The Power of an Origin Story	9
1. One Small Branch on a Large Family Tree	19
2. The Wesleyan Revival of the 1700s	23
3. The Holiness Movement	31
4. Pre-Nazarenes on the United States East Coast: The Association of Pentecostal Churches of America	39
5. Pre-Nazarenes on the United States West Coast: The Los Angeles-Based Church of the Nazarene	47
6. Pre-Nazarenes in the Southern United States: The Holiness Church of Christ	57
7. United in Holiness: The Mergers in Chicago and Pilot Point	65
Conclusion: Holiness unto the Lord Now and Forever	75

Acknowledgments

I first shared the contents of this book in a workshop presentation at the Thirtieth General Assembly and Conventions of the Church of the Nazarene in Indianapolis on June 9-10, 2023. The encouraging responses to that workshop first sparked the idea of adapting the material I shared into a book. One month later, I was afforded the wonderful opportunity to speak on Nazarene history at the Iowa District Nazarene Discipleship International (NDI) Convention on July 14, 2023. Two months after that, I shared on "Nazarene Identity" with the district superintendents of the USA/Canada Region at their District Superintendent Leadership Development Program in Louisville, Kentucky, on September 6, 2023. I included much of the same material on these occasions, and the idea for the book grew in earnest. Since then, I've shared versions of this content with Nazarene audiences at the South Central Ohio "Coaching for Effective Leadership" training on

January 13, 2023; the Kansas City District NDI "EquipKC" event on February 17, 2024; the West Texas District Vision Conference and District Assembly on April 11, 2024; the Colorado District Assembly on June 21, 2024; and the Michigan District Assembly on July 15, 2024. I owe a debt of gratitude to all those who gave me a platform for sharing this material, including R. J. Montis, Tim Carter, Eddie Estep, Sam Barber, David Downs, Virgil Askren, and Brad Dyrness.

I first floated the idea of this book to Bonnie Perry, general editor of the Church of the Nazarene. Bonnie supported my vision and encouraged me all along the way.

Jolyn Stark, Stan Ingersol, and Alex Wilson are my current colleagues at Nazarene Archives. They kept things going in the office while I devoted time to writing. It's a privilege to serve with them and with the rest of the terrific team in the office of the general secretary.

And last but certainly not least, the team at The Foundry Publishing was a delight to work with from start to finish. Many thanks to Richard Buckner, Rene McFarland, Julie Kunkle, and everyone else at the Foundry who had a hand in bringing this project to completion.

Introduction
The Power of an Origin Story

Imagine you work at an auto repair shop. The name of the shop is Bresee and Friends Automotive. It's located in Denton, Texas, just north of the Dallas metroplex. You've been working at Bresee and Friends for a few months, but all you've been able to gather so far about the name "Bresee" is that he was the person who apparently started the shop several decades ago. Other than that, you have no idea who he was, where he was from, or why he went into the auto repair business. That information, however, doesn't really seem to matter to anyone else who works at Bresee and Friends. It was a long time ago. The other employees, just like you, are simply here to make a living fixing cars.

One thing you truly appreciate about working at Bresee and Friends is that it is a first-class auto shop. It has five bays to accommodate the fast-paced and high-demand business it receives. Virtually all the equipment in the shop is brand-new, industry-standard, state-of-the-art equipment. All of it, that is, except for one curious piece of equipment in bay number one. When you started working at Bresee and Friends a few months ago, one of the things you noticed right away was that the car lift in bay number one looked totally outdated compared to the other four. The lifts in bays number two, three, four, and five look shiny and new, as if they were manufactured and installed just yesterday. And they work like it too. They're incredibly easy to maneuver. Cars zoom up and down them all day with the easy flip of a switch, which is ideal because Bresee and Friends is a super busy shop.

But the lift in bay number one is different. It actually looks like an antique. It looks like something that might be more suitable in a museum or maybe even a junkyard. It never gets used, even though all the tools and equipment around it look just as sharp and top quality as the rest of the shop. This strikes you as really odd. There must be an explanation for it. If the old lift in bay number one did get used or, better yet, totally replaced with a new one like the other four, Bresee and

Introduction

Friends could fix a lot more cars and make a lot more money.

Back during your first week on the job, as you were working under the hood each day, you started asking your coworkers: "Hey, what's up with the old lift in bay number one?" One of them replied, "I don't really know. I think it may not work, and I guess they just never got around to replacing it." Another said, "I thought I heard something about a budget crunch when they were putting the new ones in, so they just went with four. I imagine they'll probably do the fifth one at some point." Still another responded, "Huh. I guess I never really thought about it. I work in bay number five pretty much every day. I don't really ever go over to the other side of the shop."

Well, after months of receiving these same kinds of answers, your curiosity finally gets the best of you. So one day you decide to pop into the owner's office. Her name is Miss Mary Lee. She's a great lady with an open-door policy, so you knock on the door and peek your head in.

"Hey, Miss Mary Lee, I have a quick question. This may be silly, but it's been nagging at me since I started working here. What's the story with that old car lift in bay number one?"

Miss Mary Lee looks up at you, and then she slowly leans back in her chair as she relaxes her hands behind her head. With a deep sigh and a smile, she answers, "You know, it's been a long time since someone asked me about old Hiram."

"Hiram?" you reply.

"Yes," she says. "That piece of machinery actually has a name. Why don't you take a seat for a moment and let me tell you about him."

And for the next few minutes, Miss Mary Lee proceeds to tell you the origin story of Bresee and Friends Automotive. You learn that the name "Bresee" was the last name of Miss Mary Lee's grandfather. Grandpa Bresee opened the shop. He passed it along to his son, who then passed it along to his daughter, Miss Mary Lee. Grandpa Bresee opened the original shop decades ago in a smaller North Texas town not far from Denton called Pilot Point. He liked tinkering with cars from the time he was a kid helping his dad, but he didn't have any desire to open up a shop until he went off to fight in the war. While he was stationed overseas, he became quick friends with two of his comrades-in-arms, Hiram and JB, and he discovered that they really liked to tinker with cars too. They talked often, even in the trenches, about how fantastic it would be to open up

Introduction

a car shop together if they made it home. Well, tragically, his two buddies didn't make it home, but Grandpa Bresee did, and shortly after he got home to Pilot Point, he opened up the shop.

Now, at this point, as Miss Mary Lee is telling you the story, she points out her office window to bay number one and says, "Grandpa Bresee could only afford one car lift. That lift is the original one from the original shop over in Pilot Point." She continued: "You may have also noticed that the 'Bresee and Friends' sign out front looks pretty rustic and faded too. That's the original sign from the original shop. Grandpa named that sign 'JB,' and he named the lift 'Hiram.' When dad moved the shop over here to Denton, he brought both the sign and the lift with him. Grandpa told my dad, 'I may not have been able to bring Hiram and JB back from overseas with me, but *a part of them will always be a part of our shop.*'"

With those words, little tears began to well up in Miss Mary Lee's eyes and in yours as well. You thanked Miss Mary Lee for the story, moved to get up from your seat, and made your way toward the door to go back to work. But she stopped you. "Oh, just one more thing," she said. "That old car lift may look like an antique, but it actually works just fine. In fact, in all the history of Bresee and

Friends Automotive, there's never been a time when it *didn't* work!"

Introducing Institutional Memory

OK, now let's move back into real life and unpack this little imaginative story. What your coworkers in the story were not able to offer you, and what Miss Mary Lee *was* able to offer you, is a concept historians, sociologists, and organizational leaders refer to as "institutional memory." According to the Society of American Archivists' *Dictionary of Archives Terminology*, institutional memory refers to "the information held in employees' personal recollections and experiences that provides an understanding of the history and culture of an organization, especially the stories that explain the reasons behind certain decisions and procedures."[1] In our story, Miss Mary Lee had a good sense of institutional memory. Your coworkers did not, and neither did you until you went and talked to Miss Mary Lee. What you learned from her was information and context that provided you with an understanding of some

---

1. *Dictionary of Archives Terminology*, "institutional memory," accessed May 13, 2024, https://dictionary.archivists.org/entry/institutional-memory.html.

Introduction

of the history and culture of Bresee and Friends Automotive. You acquired a backstory that explained the reason behind why that old car lift was still out in bay number one.

The concept of institutional memory is important in the book you are reading because it has always been important to the Church of the Nazarene. The denomination began with a strong sense of the value of history. Early Nazarenes with Methodist roots (which were many of them) understood the Church of the Nazarene as a more authentic expression of a historic methodism that the Methodists themselves had abandoned. The Third General Assembly, in 1911, just three short years after the denomination was officially established in Pilot Point, Texas, elected E. F. Walker to serve as "general historian" for the church. This was an actual title. Regional historians were elected from the American East Coast Nazarenes, West Coast Nazarenes, and the Southern Nazarene groups to assist Walker.[2] In 1932, the Eighth General Assembly authorized the general secretary "to collect from every section of the country

---

2. The record of this is published in the *Proceedings of the Third General Assembly of the Pentecostal Church of the Nazarene* (Los Angeles: Nazarene Publishing Company, 1911), 30.

all available historic material relating to the rise and development of the denomination."[3] That authorization occurred two years *before* the United States congress passed an act establishing the National Archives of the United States of America!

For the next thirty years or so after that, the office of the general secretary continued to solicit and collect historical materials. In 1979, the Church of the Nazarene saw so much value in having a clear recollection of its institutional memory that it hired its first full-time archivist to manage a department within the office of the general secretary called Nazarene Archives. This department has served the denomination all these years because the denomination has always believed that one of the keys to fulfilling its mission is to remember where it has come from and why God raised it up in the first place.

My hope for this book is that it will provide you with a stronger sense of institutional memory about the Church of the Nazarene. I hope it will remind you, or perhaps inform you for the first

---

[3]. The record of this authorization is published in the *Journal of the Eighth General Assembly of the Church of the Nazarene* (Kansas City: Nazarene Publishing House, 1932), 167.

Introduction

time, of how the Church of the Nazarene began and why God raised it up in the first place.

So without further ado, allow me to put my "Miss Mary Lee" hat on and tell you the origin story of the Church of the Nazarene.

1

One Small Branch on a Large Family Tree

Determining where exactly to begin answering the question of how the Church of the Nazarene began is not as simple as it might seem. While the denomination officially points to the action of the Second General Assembly in Pilot Point, Texas, in 1908 for its founding, the facts of history are that many of the individuals, local churches, and institutions that would eventually make up the Church of the Nazarene were making important contributions to Nazarene history long before then. In fact, it would not be wrong to say that Nazarene history actually begins with the people of God mentioned in the Holy Scriptures. I say this because the Church of the Nazarene has always considered itself to be a branch of historic Christianity. This is clear from the opening words of the "Historical Statement" in the *Manual* of the Church of the Nazarene:

> The Church of the Nazarene confesses itself to be a branch of Christ's "one, holy, universal, and apostolic" church, embracing as its own the history of God's people recorded in the Old and New Testaments and God's people through the ages, in all expressions of Christ's church. Our denomination receives the creeds of the first five Christian centuries as expressions of its own faith. We identify with the historic church in preaching the Word, administering the sacraments, maintaining a ministry of apostolic faith and practice, and inculcating the disciplines of Christlike living and service.[1]

This statement teaches that the Church of the Nazarene identifies itself as standing in continuity with the people of God mentioned in the Christian Scriptures and with all those who have stood in that same line throughout the ages. Nazarene history is church history, and church history stretches back across the centuries to the actions

---

1. *Manual, Church of the Nazarene 2023* (Kansas City: Nazarene Publishing House, 2023), 16.

recorded in the pages of the sixty-six books of the Old and New Testaments.

General Superintendent T. Scott Daniels touched on this point in an article he wrote for *Holiness Today* in 2022. He put it like this:

> What happened to our ancestors in the faith has happened to us. Their story is now our story. This, I believe, is the primary reason Christians should continue to read and meditate on the scriptures Christians refer to as the Old Testament. We read the Old Testament to root our story, the story of Jesus, and the story of the early church in the grand story of God's redemptive activity in Israel. What God did for our ancestors God has done for us.[2]

According to this statement, it is right to affirm that Nazarene history stretches back to over two thousand years. The history of the people of God recorded in the Holy Scriptures is *Nazarene* history. The Apostles' Creed and the Nicene Creed are *Nazarene* creeds, both of which were published in the most recent edition of the Nazarene hym-

---

2. T. Scott Daniels, "How to Read the Old Testament," *Holiness Today*, September/October 2022, 10.

nal.[3] Every time Nazarenes partake of the Lord's Supper or baptize a new believer, they are doing a very *Nazarene* thing. And the reason why all of these things are very Nazarene things is because all of them are very *Christian* things.

One of the core values of the Church of the Nazarene is that Nazarenes are "a Christian people."[4] The Church of the Nazarene is a small, relatively young branch, connected to a very large, very old, and very precious family tree. If this small branch is to keep growing healthy and strong, it will be because it stayed firmly rooted to Christ's "one holy universal and apostolic church."

---

3. See *Sing to the Lord* (Kansas City: Lillenas, 1993), nos. 8, 14.

4. You can find the Church of the Nazarene's core values here: Church of the Nazarene, "Core Values," accessed June 30, 2023, https://nazarene.org/who-we-are/core-values.

2
The Wesleyan Revival of the 1700s

If this were a bigger book, we could take a deep dive into every era of church history and try to trace the Church of the Nazarene's historic connection with it. Since we don't have space for that, I'm going to do what virtually all Nazarene historians do when they talk about Nazarene history, which is fast-forward to some of the larger limbs of the tree that the small Nazarene branch hangs on. The first of those large limbs budded about seventeen hundred years after the time of Jesus Christ, in the form of a movement known as the Wesleyan Revival.

During the 1700s, a revival movement broke out in England through the ministry of two brothers, John and Charles Wesley. Both men were ordained ministers in the Church of England, or what is commonly referred to as the Anglican Church. The Wesleys and their co-laborers traveled on horseback to minister in churches, public buildings, and open fields throughout the United Kingdom. Through their ministry, scores of people repented of their sins, found salvation in Jesus Christ, and were inspired to devote themselves to Christian service. Many of these people became involved in the work of the revival itself. They joined local groups of accountable discipleship known as "societies," "class meetings," and "bands." These groups roughly correspond to what we might think of today as local churches, Sunday school classes, or small groups, except they seem to have been much more organized, intensive, and "methodical" in nearly every way. All of these things—the preaching, the meetings, and the discipleship classes—were in service to the ideals of intentionally having a holy heart and living a holy life.

As far as Christian beliefs go, the engine of the Wesleyan Revival essentially ran on three major points of emphasis. First, the Wesleys emphasized *justification by grace through faith*. They heartily affirmed the words of the fifth chapter of the Letter to the Romans: "Therefore, since we have been justified through faith, we have peace with God through our Lord Jesus Christ" (v. 1, NIV). Justification by faith was the subject of the very first sermon John Wesley published in his famous *Sermons on Several Occasions*, a sermon titled "Salvation by Faith." Wesley emphasized there and elsewhere in his preaching that God grants a full pardon and acceptance as righteous to all who believe in Jesus Christ as their Lord and Savior.

John Wesley

Second, the Wesleys emphasized *sanctification*, or *Christian perfection*, *by grace through faith*. This was a major distinctive belief for them. They preached that God not only cancels sin by forgiving it but also could *break the power* of canceled sin over a person's life. In doing so, that person, with the help of the Holy Spirit, could make progress in living a life that looked more and more like Jesus's life, more and more Christlike.

Charles Wesley

Third, the Wesleys emphasized that the Holy Spirit graciously gives believers *assurance* of their salvation and sanctification. This was John Wesley's own experience as he was attending a meeting on Aldersgate Street in London on May 24, 1738:

> In the evening I went very unwillingly to a society in Aldersgate-Street, where one was reading Luther's preface to the Epistle to the Romans. About a quarter before nine, while he was describing the change which God works in the heart through faith in Christ, I felt my heart strangely warmed. I felt I did trust in Christ, Christ alone for salvation: And an assurance was given me, that he had taken away *my* sins, even *mine*, and saved *me* from the law of sin and death.[1]

The Wesleys did not believe in the more Calvinistic doctrine of "eternal security," but they did believe in assurance. Similar to what happened to John Wesley on Aldersgate Street, they believed that the Holy Spirit "bears witness" or "gives an

---

1. John Wesley, Journal entry for May 24, 1738, in *The Works of John Wesley*, ed. Thomas Jackson, 3rd ed. (London: Wesleyan Methodist Book Room, 1872; repr., Grand Rapids: Baker, 1979), 1:103.

assurance" to individuals of God's saving and sanctifying work in their lives.

The Wesleyan Revival spread across the world. The movement came to be known as "Methodism," and in 1784 the Methodist Episcopal Church was organized in North America. The first two general superintendents of the Church of the Nazarene, Phineas F. Bresee and Hiram F. Reynolds, were ordained elders in the Methodist Episcopal Church. In fact, Bresee's Methodist ordination certificates are still preserved today at the Nazarene Archives. Bresee was ordained a deacon on September 12, 1859, by Matthew Simpson, a bishop in the Methodist Episcopal Church. Two years later, on August 25, 1861, Bresee was ordained an elder in the Methodist Episcopal Church by Bishop Levi Scott. Both ministerial credentials were recognized in 1895 by the local Church of the Nazarene in Los Angeles, where Bresee would serve as a founding pastor. There is no indication that either one was ever replaced with an ordination certificate from the Church of the Nazarene. Bresee's Methodist Episcopal Church ordination credentials, issued to him in the early years of his ministry, were deemed wholly sufficient to identify him as an ordained minister. They serve today as a tangible reminder of the Church of the

Nazarene's connection with historic Christianity in general and with the Wesleyan Revival of the 1700s in particular. This connection is part of what Nazarenes mean today when they identify themselves as standing in the "Wesleyan-Holiness" tradition.[2]

---

2. You can read more about Phineas Bresee's ordination certificates in a story I wrote for *Nazarene News*: "Nazarene Archives Highlights Original Ordination Certificates of Phineas Bresee," *Nazarene News*, May 12, 2022, https://nazarene.org/article/nazarene-archives-highlights-original-ordination-certificates-phineas-bresee.

3

The Holiness Movement

John Wesley died in 1791. Just one year before his death, in the year 1790, Wesley wrote a letter to his friend Robert Carr Brackenbury. In that letter Wesley inked these words:

> I am glad brother D– has more light with regard to full sanctification. This doctrine is the grand depositum which God has lodged with the people called Methodists; and for the sake of propagating this chiefly he appeared to have raised us up.[1]

These words are telling. They suggest that while the Wesleyan Revival certainly emphasized jus-

---

1. John Wesley, Letter to Robert Carr Brackenbury, September 15, 1790, in *Works of John Wesley*, 13:9.

tification and assurance, John Wesley himself came to believe toward the end of his life that the main reason why the Holy Spirit birthed the Wesleyan Revival was to spread the message of "full sanctification."

Approximately forty years after Wesley died, as Methodism continued to spread throughout Europe and North America, a resurgence of interest in this idea of "full sanctification," or what was also referred to as "holiness," emerged in the 1830s. One of the influences of this resurgence was a newspaper edited by Timothy Merritt of Boston, titled the *Guide to Holiness*. This was the first periodical in the United States devoted to promoting the message of holiness. In the same region of the country, another major influence emerged through the ministry of a Methodist lay preacher named Phoebe Palmer. Although she was a layperson, Palmer was nevertheless one of the most significant preachers in the world in the 1800s. From 1840 until her death in 1874, Palmer led a Tuesday gathering at her home in New York City called the Tuesday Meeting for the Promotion of Holiness. This weekly gathering was enormously popular. Palmer used it and other speaking engagements to promote this message of full sanctification.

Phoebe Palmer

Part of the appeal of Phoebe Palmer's teaching on holiness was the clarity she brought through what she referred to as a "shorter way" to attain holiness as a spiritual state.[2] This "way" involved four clear elements:

---

2. Phoebe Palmer, *The Way of Holiness, with Notes by the Way* (New York: Piercy and Reed, 1843), 1.

1. An acknowledgment of God's requirement and provision for holiness as revealed in the holy Scriptures
2. A decisive moment of "entire consecration" or "full surrender" of one's whole life to God
3. An absolute "trust" in the scriptural promises that God would accept and entirely sanctify anyone who devotes their whole life to God
4. A personal testimony to others of one's personal experience of this moment of entire sanctification

Palmer received some pushback from some Methodist clergy about this simplified teaching. But its major effect was that it made the message of holiness more understandable to ordinary people.[3]

At the same time, running parallel with Palmer's influence was an interdenominational camp meeting held in June of 1867 in the well-known Methodist community of Vineland, New Jersey. An advertisement for the camp meeting read, "The *special* objects [i.e., objectives] of this meeting will

---

3. You can read more about Phoebe Palmer's life and theology in Floyd Cunningham, ed., with Stan Ingersol, Harold E. Raser, and David P. Whitelaw, *Our Watchword and Song: The Centennial History of the Church of the Nazarene* (Kansas City: Beacon Hill Press of Kansas City, 2009), 41–46.

be to offer united and continued prayer for the revival of the work of holiness in the Church."⁴ Several thousand people attended this camp meeting. It was highly successful. It inspired more camp meetings as well as numerous local, state, and regional parachurch holiness associations. From all of this emerged an organization called the National Camp Meeting Association for the Promotion of Holiness. The organization's first president was a man named John Inskip, a Methodist minister who experienced entire sanctification under the ministry of none other than Phoebe Palmer.

An Early Holiness Camp Meeting

---

4. This was recorded in an insert with the heading "General Camp-Meeting" carried in *Guide to Holiness* in July 1867. See Cunningham et al., *Our Watchword and Song*, 47.

John Inskip

The National Camp Meeting Association for the Promotion of Holiness became a major force in the spread of the message of holiness across the United States. Through its influence, "holiness people," people who had experienced the grace of entire sanctification at camp and revival meetings and were committed to holiness of heart and life, started dotting the landscape of North America. Thus, what became known as the "Holiness Movement" of the late nineteenth and early twentieth centuries was born.

The Holiness Movement

The Holiness Movement manifested itself in broad geographical groups, or geographical "streams" of holiness people. Christian groups from three of those streams—one existing primarily on the American Atlantic coast, another on the American Pacific coast, and another bubbling up in the American South near the Gulf of Mexico—eventually merged to form the denomination known today as the Church of the Nazarene.

4

Pre-Nazarenes on the United States East Coast
The Association of Pentecostal Churches of America

The Atlantic coast stream was known as the Association of Pentecostal Churches of America.[1] The word "Pentecostal" in this context, as for other pre-Nazarene groups, did not carry the same connotations that it might today. For these pre-Nazarenes, the term "Pentecostal" was simply synonymous with the word "holiness." It was

---

1. Much of the content in this chapter is drawn from my article "The Association of Pentecostal Churches of America," *Holiness Today*, January/February 2024, 29.

a term that expressed the experience of holiness of heart and life.

People's Evangelical Church

The earliest organization within this East Coast group went by the name of the Central Evangelical Holiness Association. This was the oldest organized parent body of the present-day Church of the Nazarene. It consisted of approximately ten local churches and smaller associations scattered across America's New England states. The first of the churches was the People's Evangelical Church in Providence, Rhode Island, organized by Fred A. Hillery on July 21, 1887, with fifty-one charter members. The People's Evangelical Church stands as the oldest local church brought into the Church of the Nazarene at Pilot Point in 1908. In 1890, this congregation united with a few other independent churches and associations to form the Central Evangelical Holiness Association. The association's statement of purpose read as follows: "to promote scriptural holiness by united counsel and action, and give strength and encouragement to all those who from loyalty to this divinely inspired truth are without the privileges of real Christian fellowship."[2]

Fred A. Hillery

---

2. *Report of the Central Evangelical Holiness Association* (Providence, RI: Office of Beulah Christian, 1894), 20.

WHY GOD RAISED US UP

Shortly after the formation of the Central Evangelical Holiness Association, in January 1894 a businessman by the name of William Howard Hoople established a mission in Brooklyn, New York. Five months later, an independent church with thirty-two members was planted out of the mission. The name of that church was the Utica Avenue Pentecostal Tabernacle. Hoople served as its pastor. Over the next two years, two more churches in Brooklyn were planted: the Bedford Avenue Pentecostal Tabernacle and the Emmanuel Pentecostal Church. On December 12, 1895, Pastor Hoople organized these three churches under the name of the Association of Pentecostal Churches of America. At the organizational meeting that day they adopted the following resolution: "We will cheerfully contribute of our earthly means as God has prospered us, for the support of a faithful ministry among us, for the relief of the poor, and for the spread of the Gospel over the earth."[3]

---

3. *Beulah Christian*, April 2, 1902, 3, cited in Mendell Taylor, *Fifty Years of Nazarene Missions*, vol. 1, *Administration and Promotion* (Kansas City: Beacon Hill Press, 1952), 11.

William H. Hoople

Utica Avenue Pentecostal Tabernacle

Bedford Avenue Pentecostal Tabernacle

Annual Meeting of the Association of
Pentecostal Churches of America

Other churches joined with this cluster of Brooklyn churches, including those of the Central Evangelical Holiness Association. A minister who would eventually join the Utica Avenue Pentecostal Tabernacle was a young Methodist preacher named Hiram F. Reynolds. Reynolds served as the home and foreign missionary secretary for the Association of Pentecostal Churches of America. Under his leadership, the association established international ministry in India in 1899, in Cabo Verde in 1901, and in Canada in 1902. In Cabo Verde, the João José Dias Temple, also known as the Chapel of Ponta Achada, was built in 1909 under the leadership of João José Dias, a native of Cabo Verde who immigrated to the United States in 1889. Dias eventually settled in Providence, Rhode Island, and joined the People's Evangelical Church. With their promised support, Dias decided to return to Cabo Verde as a missionary to his homeland. In 1901, he and a few companions sailed for Cabo Verde and began work there, which included organizing churches, starting and operating a school, preaching the message of holiness, and suffering intense persecution. Their resilient faith eventually led to the construction of the historic building that bears Dias's name. It is the Church of the Nazarene's oldest building in Africa. In June 2023, it was designated as a historic landmark at the Church of the Nazarene's Thirtieth General Assembly.[4]

In North America, by 1907 the Association of Pentecostal Churches of America had a presence stretching as far east as the province of Nova Scotia in Canada to as far west as state of Iowa in the United States. When this group merged with the Church of the Nazarene, Hiram Reynolds was elected as the denomination's second general superintendent.

---

4. You can read more about João José Dias and the João José Dias Temple in a story I wrote for *Nazarene News*: "Cabo Verde Church Becomes Historic Landmark," *Nazarene News*, July 27, 2023, https://nazarene.org/article/cabo-verde-church-becomes-historic-landmark.

5

Pre-Nazarenes on the United States West Coast
The Los Angeles-Based Church of the Nazarene

While the Association of Pentecostal Churches of America was growing on the Atlantic coast, on the opposite side of the country the opening service of the first local congregation with "Church of the Nazarene" in its name took place in Los Angeles on Sunday, October 6, 1895. The gathering happened at 11:00 a.m. in a small, rented lodge hall known as Red Men's Hall. The little lodge hall was located at 317 South Main Street in downtown Los Angeles. Phineas F. Bresee, a copastor of this new church and later the first general superintendent of the Church of the Nazarene, preached to a packed house that day.

Phineas F. Bresee

We know about this service from a few historical sources. One is an actual written notice that announced the gathering to prospective attendees. As far as we know, no physical copies of the notice survive today, but its wording was transcribed verbatim and recorded by E. A. Girvin in his early biography of Bresee. Girvin was a friend and a colleague of Bresee. He published his firsthand account of Bresee's life just one year after Bresee died. In his book, Girvin noted that a copy of the written notice announcing the first service was preserved (in his time), and he recorded its contents word for word. Here's what it said:

NOTICE OF FIRST MEETING

Los Angeles, Cal., Oct., 1895.

DEAR FRIENDS:

Permit us to inform you that Rev. P. F. Bresee, D.D., will preach next Sabbath, October 6th, at 11 a.m., in the hall at 317 South Main street, Los Angeles, Cal., instead of at Peniel Hall as heretofore.

There will be a special holiness meeting at the same place at 3 p.m., conducted by Rev. J. A. Wood, D.D.

Rev. J. P. Widney, LL. D., will preach at 7:30 p.m.

We are also very glad to be able to announce to you that Drs. Widney and Bresee have arranged to associate themselves, together with such Christian people as may desire to join with them to carry on Christian work, especially evangelistic and city mission work, and the spreading of the doctrine and experience of Christian holiness.

We cordially invite you to the opening services of this work next Sabbath, October 6, 1895, at 317 S. Main street, Los Angeles, Cal.

Committee.[1]

This was the first printed advertisement for a local church with "Church of the Nazarene" in its name. For Nazarenes today, it may be worth reflecting on what they were advertising: friends to gather with, a place to hear the preaching of good news, and ministries focused on the work of evangelism, compassion, and spreading the message of Christian holiness.

Another remarkable source of information about this opening service is a newspaper report published in the *Los Angeles Daily Times* on October 7, 1895—the day after the service! That

---

1. E. A. Girvin, *Phineas F. Bresee: A Prince in Israel* (Kansas City: Nazarene Publishing House, 1916), 103. For more on the written notice, see my article "The Notice of the Opening Service of the Church of the Nazarene," *Holiness Today*, March/April 2023, 35.

Monday, the local newspaper contained breaking news:

> The first service of the new church was held in Red Men's Hall on South Main street yesterday morning. The hall was filled with worshipers, the sermon of the morning being delivered by Dr. Bresee, who spoke from the words of the prophet Jeremiah: "Thus saith the Lord, Stand ye in the ways and see and ask for the old paths, where is the good way, and walk therein, and ye shall find rest to your souls."[2]

The Scripture passage from Jeremiah is the King James Version of Jeremiah 6:16. The report went on to quote part of Dr. Bresee's sermon in which he commented on this verse: "We are to ask for the old paths. Anything new in religion is false, and yet everything in salvation is marvelously new to him who finds it."[3]

The newspaper account also noted that "no name has yet been decided upon for the new organization." In less than two weeks, however, a decision was made. In a follow-up *Los Angeles Daily Times* article covering the official organizational

---

2. "Drs. Bresee and Widney Will Found a New Church," *Los Angeles Daily Times*, October 7, 1895, 6.

3. "Drs. Bresee and Widney," 6.

service of this new church on October 20, a reporter indicated that the word "Nazarene" came to J. P. Widney, Bresee's copastor, one morning after a full night of prayer. Widney allegedly declared to the audience that Sunday that the name "Nazarene" represented "the toiling, lowly mission of Christ" and that it was "the name which was used in derision of Him by His enemies . . . the great toiling, struggling, sorrowing heart of the world. It is Jesus, Jesus of Nazareth, to whom the world in its misery and despair turns, that it may have hope."[4]

This new church plant continued to gather in Red Men's Hall for a few more weeks. On Thanksgiving Day, however, they held their first service in a different rented hall.[5] According to Girvin, the reason they had to find a new location was because "the songs of praise and shouts of triumph in this hall were distasteful to its irreligious owners."[6]

---

4. "Opening Service of the Church of the Nazarene," *Los Angeles Daily Times*, October 21, 1895, cited in Timothy L. Smith, *Called unto Holiness, The Story of the Nazarenes: The Formative Years* (Kansas City: Nazarene Publishing House, 1962), 111, 365. Also cited in Donald P. Brickley, *Man of the Morning: The Life and Work of Phineas F. Bresee* (Kansas City: Nazarene Publishing House, 1960), 135.

5. See Girvin, *Prince in Israel*, 105.

6. Girvin, 104.

Joseph P. Widney

The church rented the new hall until the next spring when they built their first structure. Some referred to the new building as "the Tabernacle." Others have called it the "Glory Barn." Girvin described it in this way: "This building was simply a board structure with sides and a roof, but in the mild climate of Southern California, it was sufficiently comfortable. It would seat about 400 people. . . . This building [was] little more than a great barn."⁷ The Glory Barn was intended to serve as a temporary gathering space until the church could build a brick-and-mortar building, but they ended up meeting in it for the next seven years!

The Glory Barn

A year and a half after the first meeting in Red Men's Hall, in January of 1897, the second Church of the Nazarene was organized in Berkeley, California. Three months after that a third one was organized in Oakland, California. In the years that followed, the Los Angeles-based Church of

---

7. Girvin, 107.

the Nazarene continued to spread. By 1907 it had organized over fifty congregations from the Pacific coast to as far east as Chicago. This group also supported a mission station in Calcutta, India.

Inside the Glory Barn

6

Pre-Nazarenes in the Southern United States
The Holiness Church of Christ

While the Los Angeles-based Church of the Nazarene was spreading from the western coast and the Association of Pentecostal Churches of America was spreading from the eastern coast, a group known as the Holiness Church of Christ was spreading across the southern United States.[1] This group was the result of a merger between two smaller southern church groups: the New

---

1. Much of the content of this chapter is drawn from my article "The Holiness Church of Christ: A Nazarene Parent Organization," *Holiness Today*, March/April 2024, 35.

Testament Church of Christ and the Independent Holiness Church.

Robert Lee Harris

The older of the two, the New Testament Church of Christ, was established in 1894 by Robert Lee Harris, an itinerant evangelist. That year, Harris organized the first local congregation of the New Testament Church of Christ in Milan, Tennessee, with fourteen charter members. Harris died from tuberculosis shortly thereafter, but his wife, Mary, took up the work he started. Mary Lee Harris remarried and went by the name of Mary Lee Cagle. She was an effective preacher. Under her ministry the New Testament Church of Christ established congregations in Tennessee, Arkansas, Alabama, and Texas.

A fact worth noting about the New Testament Church of Christ is that nearly one-third of its ministers were women. It was often the case that these women received their calls to ministry under Mary Lee Cagle's influence. Long after the Church of the Nazarene had been established as a denomination, Cagle reported the following to the Hamlin District Assembly: "Our work has not been with the larger churches, but with the weak struggling ones. I have held 13 revival meetings, preached 175 times, saw 216 converted and 118 sanctified. . . . I have [visited] practically all of the churches in the district and some of them more than once."[2] Mary Lee Cagle was a delegate to every Nazarene general assembly through 1928. She was referred to in her day as the "Mother of the Holiness Movement in the West."[3]

---

2. *Proceedings of the Fourteenth Annual Assembly of the Hamlin District Church of the Nazarene* (Kansas City: Nazarene Publishing House, 1927), 29.

3. C. A. McConnell, "Editorial," *Pentecostal Advocate*, December 2, 1909, 9.

Mary Lee Cagle

The Independent Holiness Church was organized at Van Alstyne, Texas, in 1901 by a future Nazarene leader named C. B. Jernigan. Jernigan would eventually be appointed as the first Nazarene district superintendent of the Oklahoma and Kansas District. Years before that, in October 1902, the Independent Holiness Church held its first annual meeting. At that gathering, Jernigan officiated the wedding of a young, little-known, eighteen-year-old minister named J. B. Chapman. Chapman would eventually go on to be elected as the eighth general superintendent of the Church of the Nazarene. By

1903, just two years after its founding, the Independent Holiness Church had organized twenty holiness congregations in the south.

Independent Holiness Church

In 1904, in Rising Star, Texas, just southeast of Abilene, the New Testament Church of Christ united with the Independent Holiness Church to form the Holiness Church of Christ. By 1908, this southern holiness group had established congregations from as far east as Georgia to as far west as New Mexico. They also supported global mission work in India and Japan. Their headquarters was based in Pilot Point. There they had a local Holiness Church of Christ congregation, a publishing house, a Bible college, and a maternity home known as the Rest Cottage Children's Home.

WHY GOD RAISED US UP

C. B. Jernigan

The Rising Star Union in 1904

Rest Cottage Children's Home

The fourth annual gathering of the Holiness Church of Christ, which they referred to as their "general council," was scheduled to begin on October 8, 1908, in Pilot Point.

And that is why the history of the Church of the Nazarene is forever entwined with the small town of Pilot Point, Texas.

7

United in Holiness
The Mergers in Chicago and Pilot Point

In conjunction with the Fourth General Council of the Holiness Church of Christ, the newly formed Pentecostal Church of the Nazarene—which we will discuss in a moment—decided to hold its second general assembly in Pilot Point, from October 8 to October 14, 1908. Almost exactly one year earlier, from October 10 to October 17, 1907, the Association of Pentecostal Churches of America and the Los Angeles-based Church of the Nazarene met together in Chicago at Chicago First Church of the Nazarene. At that meeting, which the denomination recognizes today as the First General

Assembly, those two groups met for the first time since they officially voted to merge earlier that year. An eyewitness report of what happened in Chicago, written by a man named Robert Pierce and published in the *Nazarene Messenger*, the official publication of the Los Angeles-based Church of the Nazarene, reads as follows:

> The flood of holy joy that swept on during the opening service was a tide of blessed triumph. In the singing of that wonderful hymn, "The Home of the Soul," the congregation seemed to be filled with rapture and to be in the very presence of the loved ones in heaven. As they took one another by the hand, so filled were they with holy joy, that for many minutes it was impossible to restrain it. The waving of nearly a thousand handkerchiefs, and the repetition of chorus after chorus, was a scene the better of which we do not expect to witness this side of the pearly gates.[1]

The group that united that day in Chicago picked a name drawn from both organizations: the Pen-

---

1. Robert Pierce, "A Great and Triumphant Service," *Nazarene Messenger*, October 24, 1907, 2.

tecostal Church of the Nazarene.[2] Phineas Bresee and Hiram Reynolds were elected as the first two general superintendents.

Also in attendance at the Chicago assembly were seven invited delegates from the southern group, the Holiness Church of Christ, including C. B. Jernigan. Not long after his return from Chicago to Texas, Jernigan published the following report of what he witnessed in Chicago:

> Well, the Chicago Convention was a glorious success in every way. The spiritual power was the greatest of any convention I ever attended. There was liberty in it clear through, and not a dry song, prayer or sermon throughout the entire session. They came from the Pacific slope and the Atlantic coast, and if I had shut

---

2. The name of the denomination was changed from "Pentecostal Church of the Nazarene" to "Church of the Nazarene" by action of the Fifth General Assembly in 1919. See *Proceedings of the Fifth General Assembly of the Pentecostal Church of the Nazarene* (Kansas City: Nazarene Publishing House, 1919), 33, 102. The change was made in response to new meanings that had come to be associated with the term "Pentecostal" from which the early Nazarenes wanted to distance themselves, as well as a desire to simply shorten the church name. For a discussion from that era of these issues, see Charles A. Gibson, "The Question of Our Church Name," *Herald of Holiness*, February 12, 1919, 8.

my eyes I would have declared that I was in an old-fashioned Texas holiness camp meeting, where the fire was falling. . . . The Mason and Dixon line . . . was obliterated and we all melted together like pieces of lead in a red-hot ladle. Glory!³

Legislative Commission, First General Assembly of the Pentecostal Church of the Nazarene, Chicago, 1907

Needless to say, the response of the delegates from the Holiness Church of Christ was extremely positive. Hoping that the Holiness Church of

---

3. C. B. Jernigan, "The Church Union Convention," *Holiness Evangel*, November 1, 1907, 4.

Christ would join with the already-united Association of Pentecostal Churches of America and the Los Angeles-based Church of the Nazarene, General Superintendent Bresee announced that the Second General Assembly of the Pentecostal Church of the Nazarene would convene down south in Pilot Point, Texas. C. B. Jernigan shared that news in the official newspaper of the Holiness Church of Christ, the *Holiness Evangel*, in an article titled "Come to the Marriage":

> You are requested to be present at the marriage of the Pentecostal Church of the Nazarene and the Holiness Church of Christ, which is to take place at Pilot Point, Texas, October 8–14 where the union of these two Holiness churches will be fully consummated in joint assembly. Men and angels will be made to rejoice at this marriage. The Father, Son and Holy Ghost will bestow their blessings upon this union.[4]

---

4. C. B. Jernigan, "Come to the Marriage," *Holiness Evangel*, September 30, 1908, 2.

Entrance to the Second General Assembly,
Pilot Point, Texas, 1908

The "marriage" took place under a large white tent on Tuesday, October 13, at 10:40 a.m. The assembly proceedings record that the motion for union passed "amid great enthusiasm" and that "the burst of holy joy continued for several minutes," with "brethren of the South throwing their arms around brethren of the North, East and West."[5] In her book *Memories of Pilot Point by One Who Was There*, Johnny Hill Jernigan, C. B. Jernigan's daughter, recalled the scene that day:

---

5. *Proceedings of the Second General Assembly of the Pentecostal Church of the Nazarene* (Los Angeles: Nazarene Publishing Company, 1908), 30.

When it was announced that the vote for union was unanimous, the assembly could not contain its exuberant joy. The Mason-Dixon Line and the ugly scars of the Civil War were forgotten and the chasm between the North and South was bridged forever! The delighted delegates waved their handkerchiefs in the air as tears of joy flowed down their cheeks. Loud shouts of "Hallelujah," "Praise the Lord," "Glory to His Name," rent the air. Shaking of hands, hugs, and slaps on the back led to a grand "Hallelujah March" around the outside of the huge tent. Just how many times the Nazarenes marched round the tent no one will ever know. But their faces were aglow with joy and determination to "encircle the globe with salvation with Holiness unto the Lord."[6]

---

6. Johnny Jernigan, *Memories of Pilot Point by One Who Was There* (Kansas City: Nazarene Publishing House, 1983), 28.

WHY GOD RAISED US UP

Delegates Waving Their Hankies

The Famous Hallelujah March

This was obviously an incredible moment. One gets the impression it was forever etched into the institutional memory of those who were there that day. Fifteen years later, at the Sixth General Assembly in 1923, this moment in 1908 in Pilot

Point was considered so significant that it was officially designated as the date the denomination would point to from that time forward for its founding. The general assembly recommendation read as follows:

> We would recommend that the time when the Second General Assembly of our Church met at Pilot Point, Texas, and three streams of the "water of life" had their glorious confluence—one from the Pacific, one from the Atlantic, and one from the Gulf of Mexico—be recognized as the date when our Church wedding took place, and we were united as one people amidst scenes of rapture far transcending the possibilities of description. We would further recommend that the Board of General Superintendents be authorized and requested to fix the exact date of this great spiritual marriage and make all necessary arrangements for its proper observance throughout our Church.[7]

---

7. *Journal of the Sixth General Assembly of the Church of the Nazarene* (Kansas City: Nazarene Publishing House, 1923), 148.

WHY GOD RAISED US UP

Leaders of the Three Uniting Groups at
the Second General Assembly

For the early Nazarenes, the union of the Association of Pentecostal Churches of America, the Los Angeles-based Church of the Nazarene, and the Holiness Church of Christ represented a great spiritual marriage. Nazarene historians Floyd Cunningham, Stan Ingersol, Harold Raser, and David Whitelaw offer this comment about the action from the 1923 General Assembly: "To the delegates of 1923, many of whom had been present at Pilot Point, the events of 1908 seemed the most fitting historical marker of what the Church of the Nazarene was and what it hoped to become, a body uniting Holiness people."[8]

---

8. Cunningham et al., *Our Watchword and Song*, 161.

Conclusion
Holiness unto the Lord Now and Forever

Well, there you have it. That's how the Church of the Nazarene began. It essentially started out as a glorious confluence of three church groups who experienced floods of holy joy in worship, shared a determination to encircle the globe with the message of holiness, and wanted to come together in unity. That's the basic origin story of the Church of the Nazarene.[1]

---

1. It is not, however, the *whole* origin story. In addition to the three larger merging groups, the Pennsylvania Conference of the Holiness Christian Church also united with the Pentecostal Church of the Nazarene in September 1908, just one month before the Pilot Point assembly. A lot also happened in the wake of the 1908 General Assembly, including additional mergers of important groups such as the Pentecostal Mission based in Nashville, the Pentecostal Church of

WHY GOD RAISED US UP

As I mentioned in the introduction, my hope for this little book is that it would remind you, or perhaps inform you for the first time, of where the Church of the Nazarene came from and why God raised it up in the first place. As we draw this book to a close, let me offer a few reflections on those things in the light of our brief walk through early Nazarene history.

First, it's worth noting that the Church of the Nazarene came from groups of believers who *embraced multiple modes of expression and points of emphasis as they tried to fulfill their mission*. An early Nazarene could be passionate about singing songs of praise and letting out shouts of triumph during worship services. Another early Nazarene might be less interested in those modes of expression and more passionate about things

---

Scotland led by George Sharpe, and the Layman's Holiness Association led by future general superintendent J. G. Morrison. Much more could also have been said about the important international work of the Church of the Nazarene parent bodies, the colleges and universities they sponsored, the works of justice and mercy and compassion they engaged in, and how early Nazarene life looked "on the ground" in local churches, especially for children and teenagers. All those things will have to be discussed on another occasion, but all are a part of the Church of the Nazarene's institutional memory.

Conclusion

such as providing relief for the poor, conducting evangelistic and city mission work, and starting crisis pregnancy centers. Still another early Nazarene could sense a greater draw toward sending out and supporting global missionaries, educating ministers, and writing and publishing. In the early days, a Nazarene could prefer to embrace and emphasize any of these things over the others and still be a faithful Nazarene. The earliest Nazarenes did not express their faith in one way or emphasize just one thing. They lived out their faith in many ways, emphasized many things as they did so, and tried to make room for others to embrace modes of expression and points of emphasis that differed from their own. The Nazarene leash was a long one when it came to how they would express their faith and what they would choose to emphasize as they did so.

This, however, does not mean that there wasn't a primary thing around which the early Nazarenes were unified. There was indeed *one primary thing* around which the early Nazarenes came together. This leads to my second reflection. *All of the Church of the Nazarene's institutional memory insists that the experience of entire sanctification as a second work of grace is at the very heart of why God raised up the Church of the Nazarene.* There's a reason why the early Nazarenes were called—and why they called themselves—"holiness people." One gets the overwhelming impression that, according to them, those who live out their historic Christianity from within the Church of the Nazarene can rightly adopt (with slight modification) John Wesley's statement at this point: This doctrine is the grand depositum which God has lodged with the people called Nazarenes, and for the sake of propagating this chiefly God appeared to have raised the Nazarenes up. Like Hiram the Car Lift at Bresee and Friends Automotive, the message of holiness of heart and life will always be a part of the Nazarene shop. This message may seem to some as if it belongs in a museum, but people all over the world still testify today that it works just fine. In fact, testimonies throughout the entire history of the Church of the Nazarene suggest that there's never been a time when it *didn't* work!

I want to wrap up this book with one final reflection. From my office at the Nazarene Archives I hear a fair bit of chatter about the notion of Christian unity. There seems to be quite a bit of interest in this, both in local churches and in the denomination at large. If the Church of the Nazarene has any hope for unity in all of its contexts,

Conclusion

it may be worth asking, Where does this hope for unity lie?

That, of course, is a big question. I certainly would not want to offer simple token answers to a question of that magnitude. As I reflect on the Nazarene origin story, however, I am aware of these truths:

1. As noted above, the Church of the Nazarene's founding members embraced multiple modes of expression and points of emphasis. This did not detract from their unity.
2. The earliest Nazarenes were postured toward unity and worked toward it, even if they were not always able to achieve it in every situation. They wanted to come together. They wanted to be united.
3. The Nazarenes have always sung it and shouted it, loud and long, that holiness unto the Lord is their watchword and song, now and forever.[2]

If Nazarenes today wish to be true to the reason why God raised them up, the question of

---

2. See Lelia N. Morris, "Holiness unto the Lord," in *Sing to the Lord*, no. 503.

unity can never be separated from the answer of holiness.

On the entrance into the campground at the 1908 General Assembly in Pilot Point, the delegates were greeted with a sign on which was inscribed the words of Jesus from his prayer recorded in John 17: "Sanctify them that they all may be one" (vv. 17, 21, KJV).

On the other side of the same sign, written for the delegates to read as they exited the campground, were these words from Matthew 19:6: "What therefore God hath joined together, let not man put asunder" (KJV).

Unity in holiness. Holy unity.

This is how the Church of the Nazarene began.

May the church steward its institutional memory well.

www.ingramcontent.com/pod-product-compliance
Lightning Source LLC
Chambersburg PA
CBHW061340040426
42444CB00011B/3009